Quick
fixes from
brand.name
mixes

Publications International, Ltd.

Favorite Brand Name Recipes at www.fbnr.com

Microwave Cooking: Microwave ovens vary in wattage. Use the cooking times as guidelines and check for doneness before adding more time.

Preparation/Cooking Times: Preparation times are based on the approximate amount of time required to assemble the recipe before cooking, baking, chilling or serving. These times include preparation steps such as measuring, chopping and mixing. The fact that some preparations and cooking can be done simultaneously is taken into account. Preparation of optional ingredients and serving suggestions is not included.

Contents

Appetizers & Snacks

Hearty Nachos

Prep Time: 10 minutes   *Cook Time:* 12 minutes

1 pound ground beef
1 envelope LIPTON® RECIPE SECRETS® Onion Soup
    Mix
1 can (19 ounces) black beans, rinsed and drained
1 cup prepared salsa
1 package (8½ ounces) plain tortilla chips
1 cup shredded Cheddar cheese (about 4 ounces)

1. In 12-inch nonstick skillet, brown ground beef over medium-high heat; drain.

2. Stir in soup mix, black beans and salsa. Bring to a boil over high heat. Reduce heat to low and simmer 5 minutes or until heated through.

3. Arrange tortilla chips on serving platter. Spread beef mixture over chips; sprinkle with Cheddar cheese. Top, if desired, with sliced green onions, sliced pitted ripe olives, chopped tomato and chopped cilantro.   *Makes 8 servings*

Juicy Jell-O®

Preparation Time: **5** minutes plus refrigerating

1 cup boiling water
1 package (4-serving size) JELL-O® Brand Gelatin, any flavor
1 cup cold juice, any flavor

STIR boiling water into gelatin in medium bowl at least 2 minutes until completely dissolved. Stir in cold juice.
REFRIGERATE 4 hours or until firm.

Makes 4 (½-cup) servings

Note: Do not use fresh or frozen pineapple, kiwi, papaya or guava juice. Gelatin will not set.

Variation: For fruited Juicy JELL-O®, prepare as directed but refrigerate for just 30 minutes until slightly thickened. Stir in 1 cup raspberries, blueberries or chopped strawberries. Refrigerate 4 hours or until firm.

Mini Cocktail Meatballs

1 envelope LIPTON® RECIPE SECRETS® Onion, Onion-Mushroom, Beefy Mushroom or Beefy Onion Soup Mix
1 pound ground beef
½ cup plain dry bread crumbs
¼ cup dry red wine or water
2 eggs, slightly beaten

1. Preheat oven to 375°F.

2. In medium bowl, combine all ingredients; shape into 1-inch meatballs.

3. In shallow baking pan, arrange meatballs and bake 18 minutes or until done. Serve, if desired, with assorted mustards or tomato sauce. *Makes about 48 meatballs*

Tortilla Crunch Chicken Fingers

    1 envelope LIPTON® RECIPE SECRETS® Savory Herb with Garlic Soup Mix

    1 cup finely crushed plain tortilla chips or cornflakes (about 3 ounces)

  1½ pounds boneless, skinless chicken breasts, cut into strips

    1 egg

    2 tablespoons water

    2 tablespoons margarine or butter, melted

1. Preheat oven to 400°F.

2. In medium bowl, combine savory herb with garlic soup mix and tortilla chips. In large plastic bag or bowl, combine chicken and egg beaten with water until evenly coated. Remove chicken and dip in tortilla mixture until evenly coated; discard bag. On 15½×10½×1-inch jelly-roll pan sprayed with nonstick cooking spray, arrange chicken; drizzle with margarine. Bake, uncovered, 12 minutes or until chicken is done. Serve with chunky salsa, if desired.   *Makes about 24 chicken fingers*

Tip: Serve chicken with your favorite fresh or prepared salsa.

Original Ranch® Snack Mix

    8 cups KELLOGG'S® CRISPIX®* cereal

  2½ cups small pretzels

  2½ cups bite-size Cheddar cheese crackers (optional)

    3 tablespoons vegetable oil

    1 packet (1 ounce) HIDDEN VALLEY® The Original Ranch® Salad Dressing & Seasoning Mix

*Kellogg's® and Crispix® are registered trademarks of Kellogg Company.

Combine cereal, pretzels and crackers in a gallon-size Glad® Zipper Storage Bag. Pour oil over mixture. Seal bag and toss to coat. Add salad dressing & seasoning mix; seal bag and toss again until coated.   *Makes 10 cups*

Philadelphia® Garlic & Herb Dip

Prep Time: 5 minutes plus refrigerating

**2 package (8 ounces) PHILADELPHIA® Cream Cheese,
    softened
1 envelope GOOD SEASONS® Garlic & Herb Salad Dressing
    Mix
½ cup milk**

MIX all ingredients with electric mixer on medium speed until
well blended; cover. Refrigerate several hours or until chilled.
SERVE with assorted fresh vegetables and NABISCO® Crackers.

Makes 2½ cups

Pizza Crescents

**1½ cups (6 ounces) shredded JARLSBERG LITE™ cheese
1 (6½-ounce) bag dry pizza crust mix
½ cup water
    All-purpose flour for dusting fingers**

Toss together cheese and pizza crust mix. Stir in water until
moistened, adding a few drops of water, if necessary. Divide
dough into 6 parts, about ¼ cup each. Preheat oven to 425°F.

With clean, floured fingers, pat each dough piece into 6-inch
circle. Fill each with pizza sauce and/or assorted fillings
(suggestions follow). Fold dough over filling to create semi-
circle, pressing edges together. Place on nonstick or greased
pan; bake 15 minutes or until crisp and golden.

Makes 6 servings

Tip: Decorate with a few additional strands of shredded
Jarlsberg cheese, if desired, before baking.

Fillings: Fill each circle with 2 tablespoons pizza sauce and
1 tablespoon shredded JARLSBERG LITE™ cheese; **or**
1 tablespoon applesauce or drained canned fruit cocktail, dash
of cinnamon or clove and 1 tablespoon raisins or chopped dried
fruit; **or** 2 tablespoons ½-inch-dice hard tofu, 2 tablespoons
chopped green onions, leftover cooked vegetables (such as
string beans, broccoli, corn) and ¼ teaspoon light soy sauce.

Party Stuffed Pinwheels

1 envelope LIPTON® RECIPE SECRETS® Savory Herb with
   Garlic Soup Mix*
1 package (8 ounces) cream cheese, softened
1 cup shredded mozzarella cheese (about 4 ounces)
1 tablespoon grated Parmesan cheese
2 tablespoons milk
2 packages (10 ounces each) refrigerated pizza crust

Also terrific with LIPTON® RECIPE SECRETS® Onion Soup Mix.

1. Preheat oven to 425°F. In medium bowl, combine all
ingredients except pizza crusts; set aside.

2. Unroll pizza crusts, then top evenly with filling. Roll, starting
at longest side, jelly-roll style. Cut into 32 rounds.*

3. On baking sheet sprayed with nonstick cooking spray, arrange
rounds cut side down.

4. Bake uncovered 13 minutes or until golden brown.

Makes 32 pinwheels

If rolled pizza crust is too soft to cut, refrigerate or freeze until firm.

Zesty Bruschetta

1 envelope LIPTON® RECIPE SECRETS® Savory Herb with
   Garlic Soup Mix
6 tablespoons olive or vegetable oil*
1 loaf French or Italian bread (about 18 inches long), sliced
   lengthwise
2 tablespoons shredded or grated Parmesan cheese

Substitution: Use ½ cup margarine or butter, melted.

1. Preheat oven to 350°F. Blend savory herb with garlic soup
mix and oil. Brush onto bread, then sprinkle with cheese.

2. Bake 12 minutes or until golden. Slice, then serve.

Makes 1 loaf, about 18 pieces

Extra Special Spinach Dip

1 envelope LIPTON® RECIPE SECRETS® Vegetable Soup
    Mix*
1 container (8 ounces) regular or light sour cream
1 cup regular or light mayonnaise
1 package (10 ounces) frozen chopped spinach, thawed and
    squeezed dry
1 can (8 ounces) water chestnuts, drained and chopped
    (optional)

*Also terrific with LIPTON® RECIPE SECRETS® Savory Herb with
Garlic Soup Mix.*

1. In medium bowl, combine all ingredients; chill at least
2 hours.
2. Serve with your favorite dippers.   *Makes 3 cups dip*

Potato Skins

4 baked potatoes, quartered
¼ cup sour cream
1 packet (1 ounce) HIDDEN VALLEY® The Original Ranch®
    Salad Dressing & Seasoning Mix
1 cup (4 ounces) shredded Cheddar cheese
    Sliced green onions and/or bacon pieces* (optional)

Crisp-cooked, crumbled bacon may be used.

Scoop potato out of skins; combine potatoes with sour cream
and salad dressing & seasoning mix. Fill skins with mixture.
Sprinkle with cheese. Bake at 375°F. for 12 to 15 minutes or
until cheese is melted. Garnish with green onions and/or bacon
pieces, if desired.   *Makes 8 to 10 servings*

Creamy Cantaloupe

Prep: 15 minutes   *Refrigerate:* 3 hours

1 medium cantaloupe (about 3½ pounds)
¾ cup boiling water
1 package (4-serving size) JELL-O® Brand Gelatin, any flavor
½ cup cold orange juice
½ cup thawed COOL WHIP® Whipped Topping

CUT melon in half lengthwise; remove seeds. Scoop out melon, leaving about 1-inch-thick border of melon. Dice scooped-out melon. Drain well. Cut thin slice from bottom of each melon shell to allow shells to stand upright, or place in small bowls.

STIR boiling water into gelatin in large bowl at least 2 minutes until completely dissolved. Stir in cold juice. Refrigerate 15 minutes or until slightly thickened (consistency of unbeaten egg whites). Gently stir in whipped topping. Stir in reserved diced melon. Pour into melon shells.

REFRIGERATE 3 hours or until firm. Cut into wedges.

Makes 8 servings

Tip: Choose a cantaloupe that is firm but yields to gentle thumb pressure at the blossom end. The melon should have a pleasant odor. Ripen cantaloupe at room temperature; refrigerate and be sure to use within 2 to 3 days.

Roasted Nuts from Hidden Valley®

1 packet (1 ounce) HIDDEN VALLEY® The Original Ranch®
　　Salad Dressing & Seasoning Mix
1 pound assorted unsalted nuts, such as pecans, walnuts or
　　mixed nuts
¼ cup maple syrup
2 tablespoons light brown sugar

Place nuts in plastic bag; add maple syrup and coat well. Sprinkle sugar and salad dressing & seasoning mix over nuts. Coat well. Spread nuts in single layer on greased baking sheet. Bake at 250°F. for 35 minutes. Transfer immediately to large bowl. Cool, stirring to separate.　　*Makes about 4 cups*

Creamy Cantaloupe

Crispy Ranch Breadsticks

2 tablespoons dry ranch party dip mix
2 tablespoons sour cream
1 package (10 ounces) refrigerated pizza dough
  Butter, melted

1. Preheat oven to 400°F. Grease baking sheets or line with parchment paper. Combine dip mix and sour cream in small bowl; set aside.

2. Unroll pizza dough on lightly floured work surface. Shape dough into 16×10-inch rectangle. Brush with melted butter. Spread dip mixture evenly over top of dough rectangle; cut into 24 (10-inch) strips. Shape into desired shapes.

3. Place breadsticks ½ inch apart on prepared baking sheets. Bake 10 minutes or until golden brown. Serve immediately or place on wire rack to cool. *Makes 24 breadsticks*

Crispy Spiced Nut Breadsticks: Place 1 cup finely chopped pecans and 1 tablespoon vegetable oil in plastic bag; toss to coat. Combine ¼ teaspoon chili powder, ¼ teaspoon ground cumin, ¼ teaspoon curry powder, ⅛ teaspoon ground cinnamon and dash of ground red pepper in small bowl. Add to nuts; toss to coat. Place nuts in small pan over medium heat and stir constantly until nuts are lightly toasted. Sprinkle nut mixture with 1 teaspoon garlic salt; cool to room temperature. Instead of spreading dough with sour cream mixture, sprinkle ½ cup spiced nuts over dough (store remaining nuts in tightly covered container). Cut into 24 (10-inch) strips. Shape into desired shapes. Bake as directed.

Top to bottom: Crispy Spiced Nut Breadsticks and Crispy Ranch Breadsticks

Soups, Salads & Sandwiches

Bouillabaisse

Prep Time: 15 minutes   *Cook Time:* 10 minutes

2 cups water
1 package KNORR® Recipe Classics™ Vegetable or Spring Vegetable Soup, Dip and Recipe Mix
1 bottle or can (8 to 10 ounces) clam juice
2 teaspoons tomato paste
½ teaspoon paprika
¼ teaspoon saffron threads (optional)
12 mussels or clams, well scrubbed
1½ pounds mixed seafood (cubed cod, snapper, scallops or shrimp)

• In 3-quart saucepan, bring water, recipe mix, clam juice, tomato paste, paprika and saffron to a boil over medium-high heat, stirring occasionally.

• Add mussels and seafood. Bring to a boil over high heat.

• Reduce heat to low and simmer **5** minutes or until shells open and seafood is cooked through and flakes easily when tested with a fork. Discard any unopened shells.

Makes 6 servings

Warm Mediterranean Rice Salad

1½ cups uncooked UNCLE BEN'S® ORIGINAL CONVERTED®
    Brand Rice
 2 teaspoons dried basil
 ½ cup red wine vinaigrette, divided
 1 can (6 ounces) solid white tuna in water, drained and flaked
 1 cup chopped green bell pepper
 1 cup chopped tomato
 ½ cup diced red onion
 ½ cup (about 18 to 20) Kalamata or pitted black olives

1. Prepare rice according to package directions. Stir basil and about ⅓ cup of vinaigrette into rice.

2. Meanwhile, combine tuna, bell pepper, tomato and red onion in large salad bowl.

3. Add rice mixture to tuna and vegetables in salad bowl. Stir in remaining vinaigrette and olives.   *Makes 6 servings*

Italian Vegetable Soup

Prep Time: 20 minutes   *Cook Time:* 25 minutes

1 package KNORR® Recipe Classics™ Tomato Basil Soup,
    Dip and Recipe Mix
4 cups water
2 cups sliced fennel or broccoli florets
1 large zucchini, diced (about 2 cups)
1 teaspoon dried oregano
   Grated Parmesan cheese (optional)

• In 4-quart Dutch oven, combine recipe mix, water, fennel, zucchini and oregano. Stirring occasionally, bring to a boil over medium-high heat.

• Reduce heat, cover and simmer 15 minutes, stirring occasionally or until vegetables are tender.

• If desired, sprinkle lightly with Parmesan cheese
              Makes 6 (1-cup) servings

Lipton® Onion Burgers

Prep Time: 10 minutes   *Cook Time:* 12 minutes

1 envelope LIPTON® RECIPE SECRETS® Onion Soup Mix*
2 pounds ground beef
½ cup water

*Also terrific with LIPTON® RECIPE SECRETS® Beefy Onion, Onion-Mushroom, Beefy Mushroom, Savory Herb with Garlic or Ranch Soup Mix.

1. In large bowl, combine all ingredients; shape into 8 patties.
2. Grill or broil until done.   *Makes about 8 servings*

Hidden Valley® Potato Salad

1 packet (1 ounce) HIDDEN VALLEY® The Original Ranch®
    Salad Dressing & Seasoning Mix
½ cup mayonnaise
¼ cup water
8 medium potatoes (boiled, peeled and cubed)
1 cup sliced celery
½ cup chopped red onion

Combine dressing mix with mayonnaise and water. Add potatoes, celery and onion. Toss to coat. Chill.   *Makes 4 to 6 servings*

Sparkling Berry Salad

Preparation Time: 15 minutes   *Refrigerating Time:* 5½ hours

2 cups boiling diet cranberry juice cocktail
1 package (8-serving size) *or* 2 packages (4-serving size)
    JELL-O® Brand Sugar Free Low Calorie Gelatin Dessert
    or JELL-O® Brand Gelatin Dessert, any red flavor
1½ cups cold seltzer or club soda
    ¼ cup creme de cassis liqueur (optional)
1 teaspoon lemon juice
3 cups assorted berries (blueberries, raspberries and sliced
    strawberries), divided

STIR boiling cranberry juice into gelatin in large bowl at least
2 minutes until completely dissolved. Stir in cold seltzer,
liqueur, if desired, and lemon juice. Refrigerate about 1½ hours
or until slightly thickened (consistency of unbeaten egg whites).

STIR in 2 cups of the berries. Spoon into 5-cup mold.

REFRIGERATE 4 hours or until firm. Unmold. Top with
remaining 1 cup berries.   *Makes 8 servings*

Cherry Waldorf Salad

1¼ cups apple juice, divided
1 package (4-serving size) JELL-O® Brand Cherry Flavor
    Sugar Free Gelatin
Ice cubes
½ cup finely chopped peeled apple
1 small banana, sliced or finely chopped
¼ cup sliced celery

BRING ¾ cup of the apple juice to a boil in medium saucepan.
Completely dissolve gelatin in boiling apple juice. Combine the
remaining ½ cup apple juice and enough ice cubes to measure
1¼ cups. Add to gelatin; stir until slightly thickened. Remove
any unmelted ice. Stir in fruit and celery. Spoon into individual
dishes or medium serving bowl. Chill until firm, about 2 hours.
                              Makes 2½ cups or 5 servings

Onion Sloppy Joes

1½ pounds ground beef
  1 envelope LIPTON® RECIPE SECRETS® Onion Soup Mix
  1 cup water
  1 cup ketchup
  2 tablespoons firmly packed brown sugar

1. In 10-inch skillet, brown ground beef over medium-high heat; drain.

2. Stir in remaining ingredients. Bring to a boil over high heat.

3. Reduce heat to low and simmer uncovered, stirring occasionally, 8 minutes or until mixture thickens. Serve, if desired, on hoagie rolls or hamburger buns.

Makes about 6 servings

Serving Suggestion: Serve with a lettuce and tomato salad, tortilla chips and ice cream with a choice of toppings.

Creamy Broccoli Noodle Soup

3½ cups milk
  1 package (10 ounces) frozen chopped broccoli
  1 pouch LIPTON® Soup Secrets Noodle Soup Mix with Real
    Chicken Broth

In medium saucepan, combine all ingredients; bring to a boil. Reduce heat and simmer uncovered, stirring occasionally, 5 minutes or until noodles are tender.

Makes 4 (1-cup) servings

Fast 'n Easy Chili

1½ pounds ground beef
1 envelope LIPTON® RECIPE SECRETS® Onion Soup Mix*
1 can (15 to 19 ounces) red kidney or black beans, drained
1½ cups water
1 can (8 ounces) tomato sauce
4 teaspoons chili powder

Also terrific with LIPTON® RECIPE SECRETS® Beefy Mushroom, Onion-Mushroom or Beefy Onion Soup Mix.

1. In 12-inch skillet, brown ground beef over medium-high heat; drain.

2. Stir in remaining ingredients. Bring to a boil over high heat. Reduce heat to low and simmer covered, stirring occasionally, 20 minutes. Top hot chili with shredded Cheddar cheese, and serve over hot cooked rice, if desired.   *Makes 6 servings*

First Alarm Chili: Add 5 teaspoons chili powder.

Second Alarm Chili: Add 2 tablespoons chili powder.

Third Alarm Chili: Add chili powder at your own risk.

Souper Stuffed Cheese Burgers

1 envelope LIPTON® RECIPE SECRETS® Onion Soup Mix*
2 pounds ground beef
½ cup water
¾ cup shredded Cheddar, mozzarella or Monterey Jack cheese (about 6 ounces)

*Also terrific with LIPTON® RECIPE SECRETS® Savory Herb with Garlic, Onion-Mushroom or Beefy Onion Soup Mix.

1. In large bowl, combine soup mix, ground beef and water; shape into 12 patties.

2. Place 2 tablespoons cheese in center of 6 patties. Top with remaining patties and seal edges tightly.

3. Grill or broil until done. Serve, if desired, on onion-poppy seed rolls.   *Makes 6 servings*

Tip: Perk up your burgers by serving them on something besides a bun. Try bagels, English muffins, pita bread, specialty rolls, or even tortillas for a fun change of pace!

Caesar Pasta Salad

Prep Time: **5** minutes   *Cook Time:* **10 minutes**

3 cups cooked pasta
1 bag (16 ounces) frozen stir-fry vegetable mixture, thawed and drained
1 cup Caesar salad dressing
¼ cup LA CHOY® Soy Sauce

In large bowl, combine all ingredients; toss to coat evenly. Cover and refrigerate until ready to serve.   *Makes 8 servings*

Top to bottom: Souper Stuffed Cheese Burger, Garlic Fries (page 68)

French Onion Soup

2 tablespoons butter
3 medium onions, thinly sliced and separated into rings
1 package (1.0 ounce) LAWRY'S® Au Jus Gravy Mix
3 cups water
4 thin slices sourdough French bread
   Unsalted butter, softened
4 slices Swiss or Gruyère cheese

In large skillet, heat 2 tablespoons butter. Add onions and cook over medium-high heat until golden. In small bowl, combine Au Jus Gravy Mix and water; add to onions. Bring to a boil over medium-high heat. Reduce heat to low; cover and simmer 15 minutes, stirring occasionally. Broil bread on one side until lightly toasted. Turn bread slices over; spread with unsalted butter. Top with cheese; broil until cheese melts.

Makes 4 servings

Serving Suggestion: To serve, pour soup into tureen or individual bowls. Top each serving with toast.

Hint: If using individual, ovenproof bowls, pour soup into bowls; top with a slice of untoasted bread. Top with cheese. Place under broiler just until cheese is melted.

Seafood Salad Sandwiches

1 envelope LIPTON® RECIPE SECRETS® Vegetable Soup
    Mix
¾ cup sour cream
½ cup chopped celery
¼ cup mayonnaise
1 tablespoon fresh or frozen chopped chives (optional)
1 teaspoon lemon juice
    Hot pepper sauce to taste
⅛ teaspoon ground black pepper
2 packages (6 ounces each) frozen crabmeat, thawed and well
    drained*
4 hard rolls, halved
    Lettuce leaves

Variations: Use 1 package (12 ounces) frozen cleaned shrimp, cooked and coarsely chopped; or 2 packages (8 ounces each) sea legs, thawed, drained and chopped; or 1 can (12 ounces) tuna, drained and flaked; or 2 cans (about 4 ounces each) medium or large shrimp, drained and chopped; or 2 cans (6 ounces each) crabmeat, drained and flaked.

In large bowl, blend vegetable soup mix, sour cream, celery, mayonnaise, chives, lemon juice, hot pepper sauce and pepper. Stir in crabmeat; chill. To serve, line rolls with lettuce, then fill with crab mixture.   *Makes 4 sandwiches*

Vegetable Potato Salad

Prep Time: 20 minutes   *Chill Time:* 2 hours

**1 envelope LIPTON® RECIPE SECRETS® Vegetable Soup
    Mix**
1 cup HELLMANN'S® or BEST FOODS® Mayonnaise
2 teaspoons white vinegar
**2 pounds red or all-purpose potatoes, cooked and cut into
    chunks**
¼ cup red onion, finely chopped (optional)

1. In large bowl, combine soup mix, mayonnaise and vinegar.
2. Add potatoes and onion; toss well. Chill 2 hours.

Makes 6 servings

15-Minute Stew

1 tablespoon olive or vegetable oil
1 pound boneless sirloin steak, cut into 1-inch cubes
1 envelope LIPTON® RECIPE SECRETS® Onion Soup Mix
1 cup water
2 tablespoons tomato paste
**1 can (14½ ounces) new potatoes, drained and cut into
    chunks**
1 package (10 ounces) frozen peas and carrots

1. In 12-inch skillet, heat oil over medium-high heat and brown
steak.

2. Stir in remaining ingredients. Bring to a boil over high heat.

3. Reduce heat to low and simmer uncovered, stirring
occasionally, 10 minutes or until steak is tender.

Makes 4 servings

One-Dish Extravaganza

Oriental Chicken & Rice

Prep Time: 5 minutes   *Cook Time:* 25 minutes

1 (6.9-ounce) package RICE-A-RONI® Chicken Flavor
2 tablespoons margarine or butter
1 pound boneless, skinless chicken breasts, cut into thin
    strips
¼ cup teriyaki sauce
½ teaspoon ground ginger
1 (16-ounce) package frozen Oriental-style mixed
    vegetables

1. In large skillet over medium heat, sauté rice-vermicelli mix with margarine until vermicelli is golden brown.

2. Slowly stir in 2 cups water, chicken, teriyaki sauce, ginger and Special Seasonings; bring to a boil. Reduce heat to low. Cover; simmer 10 minutes.

3. Stir in vegetables. Cover; simmer 5 to 10 minutes or until rice is tender and chicken is no longer pink inside. Let stand 3 minutes.   *Makes 4 servings*

Tip: Use pork instead of chicken and substitute ¼ cup orange juice for ¼ cup of the water.

Southwestern Meat Loaf

1 envelope LIPTON® RECIPE SECRETS® Onion Soup Mix*
2 pounds ground beef
2 cups (about 3 ounces) cornflakes or bran flakes cereal,
    crushed
1½ cups frozen or drained canned whole kernel corn
1 small green bell pepper, chopped
2 eggs
¾ cup water
⅓ cup ketchup

Also terrific with LIPTON® RECIPE SECRETS® Onion-Mushroom or Beefy Onion Soup Mix.

1. Preheat oven to 350°F. In large bowl, combine all ingredients.

2. In 13×9-inch baking or roasting pan, shape into loaf.

3. Bake uncovered 1 hour or until done. Let stand 10 minutes before serving. Serve, if desired, with salsa.

Makes 8 servings

Tip: For a great lunchbox treat, wrap leftover meat loaf slices in tortillas and top with your favorite taco toppings, such as salsa, sour cream, grated cheese and shredded lettuce.

Seafood Risotto

Prep Time: 5 minutes   *Cook Time:* 15 minutes

1 package (5.2 ounces) rice in creamy sauce (Risotto Milanese flavor)
1 package (14 to 16 ounces) frozen fully cooked shrimp
1 box (10 ounces) BIRDS EYE® frozen Mixed Vegetables
2 teaspoons grated Parmesan cheese

• In 4-quart saucepan, prepare rice according to package directions. Add frozen shrimp and vegetables during last 10 minutes of cooking.

• Sprinkle with cheese.   *Makes 4 servings*

Easy Chicken Pot Pie

2 cups cut-up cooked chicken
1 package (10 ounces) frozen mixed vegetables, thawed
1¼ cups milk
1 envelope LIPTON® RECIPE SECRETS® Golden Onion Soup Mix*
1 pie crust or pastry for single-crust pie

*Also terrific with LIPTON® RECIPE SECRETS® Savory Herb with Garlic Soup Mix.

1. Preheat oven to 400°F. In 9-inch pie plate, combine chicken and vegetables; set aside.

2. In small saucepan, bring milk and soup mix to a boil over medium heat, stirring occasionally. Cook 1 minute. Stir into chicken mixture.

3. Top with pie crust. Press pastry around edge of pie plate to seal; trim excess pastry, then flute edges. With tip of knife, make small slits in pastry.

4. Bake uncovered 35 minutes or until crust is golden.
                    Makes about 4 servings

Chicken Jambalaya

Prep Time: 15 minutes   *Cook Time:* 25 minutes

2 tablespoons vegetable oil
¾ pound boneless chicken thighs or breasts, cut into cubes
1 cup ham cut into very thin strips (about 5 ounces)
1 can (14½ to 16 ounces) seasoned diced tomatoes in juice,
    undrained
1½ cups water
1 can (4 ounces) diced green chilies, undrained
1 package KNORR® Recipe Classics™ Vegetable Soup,
    Dip and Recipe Mix
1 cup uncooked rice

• In large skillet, heat oil over medium-high heat and brown chicken and ham. Stir in tomatoes, water, chilies and recipe mix. Bring to a boil over high heat. Stir in rice.

• Reduce heat to low and simmer covered, stirring occasionally, 20 minutes or until rice is tender.   *Makes 4 servings*

Saucepot Spinach Lasagne

Prep Time: 20 minutes

1 package KNORR® Recipe Classics™ Leek Soup, Dip and
    Recipe Mix
3 cups water
8 ounces uncooked wide egg noodles (about 6 cups)
1 cup milk
1 package (10 ounces) frozen leaf spinach, thawed
2 cups shredded mozzarella cheese, divided (about 8 ounces)
⅓ cup grated Parmesan cheese

• In 4-quart saucepot, combine recipe mix and water. Add noodles and milk. Stirring frequently, heat to boiling. Reduce heat; stirring occasionally, simmer 5 minutes.

• Add spinach; heat to simmering. Stir in 1 cup mozzarella and the parmesan cheese. Spoon into shallow serving bowl and sprinkle with remaining mozzarella cheese.

Makes 4 servings

Savory Chicken & Biscuits

2 tablespoons olive or vegetable oil
1 pound boneless skinless chicken breasts or thighs, cut into
    1-inch pieces (about 2 cups)
1 medium onion, chopped
1 cup thinly sliced carrots
1 cup thinly sliced celery
1 envelope LIPTON® RECIPE SECRETS® Savory Herb with
    Garlic Soup Mix*
1 cup milk
1 package (10 ounces) refrigerated flaky buttermilk biscuits

*Also terrific with LIPTON® RECIPE SECRETS® Golden Onion
Soup Mix.*

1. Preheat oven to 400°F.

2. In 12-inch skillet, heat oil over medium-high heat and cook
chicken, stirring occasionally, 5 minutes or until almost done.
Stir in onion, carrots and celery; cook, stirring occasionally,
3 minutes. Stir in savory herb with garlic soup mix blended with
milk. Bring to the boiling point over medium-high heat, stirring
occasionally; cook 1 minute. Turn into lightly greased 2-quart
casserole; arrange biscuits on top of chicken mixture, with
edges touching. Bake 10 minutes or until biscuits are golden
brown.   *Makes about 4 servings*

51

Herbed Chicken & Vegetables

Prep Time: 10 minutes   *Cook Time:* 40 minutes

2 medium all-purpose potatoes, thinly sliced (about 1 pound)
2 medium carrots, sliced
4 bone-in chicken pieces (about 2 pounds)
1 envelope LIPTON® RECIPE SECRETS® Savory Herb with Garlic Soup Mix
⅓ cup water
1 tablespoon olive or vegetable oil

1. Preheat oven to 425°F. In broiler pan without the rack, place potatoes and carrots; arrange chicken on top. Pour soup mix blended with water and oil over chicken and vegetables.

2. Bake uncovered 40 minutes or until chicken is no longer pink and vegetables are tender.   *Makes 4 servings*

Slow Cooker Method: Place all ingredients in slow cooker, arranging chicken on top; cover. Cook on HIGH 4 hours or LOW 6 to 8 hours.

One-Dish Chicken Bake

Prep Time: 10 minutes   *Bake Time:* 35 minutes

1 package (6 ounces) STOVE TOP® Stuffing Mix for Chicken
4 boneless skinless chicken breast halves (about 1¼ pounds)
1 can (10¾ ounces) condensed cream of mushroom soup, undiluted
⅓ cup BREAKSTONE® or KNUDSEN® Sour Cream or milk

1. STIR stuffing crumbs, contents of Stuffing Mix Pouch, 1½ cups hot water and ¼ cup margarine, cut-up, just until moistened; set aside.

2. PLACE chicken in 12×8-inch baking dish. Mix soup and sour cream; pour over chicken. Top with stuffing.

3. BAKE at 375°F for 35 minutes or until chicken is cooked through.   *Makes 4 servings*

Chuckwagon BBQ Rice Round-Up

Prep Time: 5 minutes   *Cook Time:* 25 minutes

1 pound lean ground beef
1 (6.8-ounce) package RICE-A-RONI® Beef Flavor
2 tablespoons margarine or butter
2 cups frozen corn
½ cup prepared barbecue sauce
½ cup (2 ounces) shredded Cheddar cheese

1. In large skillet over medium-high heat, brown ground beef until well cooked; drain. Remove from skillet; set aside.

2. In same skillet over medium heat, sauté rice-vermicelli mix with margarine until vermicelli is golden brown.

3. Slowly stir in 2½ cups water, corn and Special Seasonings; bring to a boil. Reduce heat to low. Cover; simmer 15 to 20 minutes or until rice is tender.

4. Stir in barbecue sauce and ground beef. Sprinkle with cheese. Cover; let stand 3 to 5 minutes or until cheese is melted.

Makes 4 servings

Tip: Salsa can be substituted for barbecue sauce.

Chicken Mexicana Casserole

10 boneless, skinless chicken breast halves (about
       2½ pounds), cut into 1-inch cubes
  2 packages (1.0 ounce each) LAWRY'S® Taco Spices
       & Seasonings
  2 cans (14½ ounces each) whole tomatoes, undrained, cut up
  3 cups (12 ounces) shredded sharp cheddar cheese, divided
  1 can (7 ounces) diced green chiles, undrained
  1 can (12 ounces) whole kernel corn, drained
  1 package (8¼ ounces) corn muffin mix
  2 eggs
  ¼ cup sour cream

In large bowl, toss chicken cubes with Taco Spices & Seasonings
and tomatoes; mix well. Add 1 cup cheese. Spread mixture
evenly into 13×9×2-inch baking dish. Spoon chiles over chicken
mixture; sprinkle with remaining cheese. Set aside. In medium
bowl, combine remaining ingredients; mix well. Drop by
rounded spoonfuls on top of casserole, spacing evenly. Bake in
350°F oven 50 to 60 minutes or until top is lightly browned and
sauce is bubbly. Remove from oven and let stand about
20 minutes before serving.   *Makes 10 to 12 servings*

Serving Suggestion: Serve with black beans and sliced
tomatoes.

Sides of All Kinds

Vegetable Parmesan Bake

1 envelope LIPTON® RECIPE SECRETS® Garlic
    Mushroom Soup Mix
¼ cup grated Parmesan cheese
1 large baking potato, cut into ¼-inch-thick slices
1 medium zucchini, diagonally cut into ¼-inch-thick slices
1 large tomato, cut into ¼-inch-thick slices
1 tablespoon margarine or butter, cut into small pieces

1. Preheat oven to 375°F. In small bowl, combine soup mix and Parmesan cheese; set aside.

2. In shallow 1-quart casserole sprayed with nonstick cooking spray, arrange potato slices, overlapping slightly. Sprinkle with ⅓ of the soup mixture. Top with zucchini slices, overlapping slightly. Sprinkle with ⅓ of the soup mixture. Top with tomato slices, overlapping slightly. Sprinkle with remaining soup mixture. Top with margarine.

3. Bake covered 40 minutes. Remove cover and bake an additional 10 minutes or until vegetables are tender.

Makes 4 servings

Tip: For delicious tomatoes any time of the year, store them on your kitchen counter out of direct sunlight. Never store them in the refrigerator, since this can spoil their flavor and texture.

Southwestern Rice

1 cup uncooked converted rice
1 can (15 ounces) black beans, rinsed and drained
1 can (8 ounces) corn, drained
1 packet (1 ounce) HIDDEN VALLEY® The Original Ranch®
    Salad Dressing & Seasoning Mix
¾ cup (3 ounces) diced Monterey Jack cheese
½ cup seeded, diced tomato
¼ cup sliced green onions

Cook rice according to package directions, omitting salt. During last five minutes of cooking time, quickly uncover and add beans and corn; cover immediately. When rice is done, remove saucepan from heat; add salad dressing & seasoning mix and stir. Let stand 5 minutes. Stir in cheese, tomato and onions. Serve immediately.   *Makes 6 servings*

Original Ranch® Grilled Bread

1 packet (1 ounce) HIDDEN VALLEY® The Original Ranch®
    Salad Dressing & Seasoning Mix
½ cup butter
2 loaves French bread, cut in half lengthwise

Soften butter and stir in dressing mix. Spread on bread. Grill or broil until golden.   *Makes 2 loaves*

Mozzarella Bread Variation: Sprinkle ½ cup shredded mozzarella cheese on top before grilling or broiling.

Original Ranch® Roasted Potatoes

2 pounds small red potatoes, quartered
¼ cup vegetable oil
1 packet (1 ounce) HIDDEN VALLEY® The Original Ranch®
 Salad Dressing & Seasoning Mix

Place potatoes in a gallon-size Glad® Zipper Storage Bag. Pour oil over potatoes. Seal bag and toss to coat. Add salad dressing & seasoning mix; seal bag and toss again until coated. Bake in ungreased baking pan at 450°F. for 30 to 35 minutes or until potatoes are brown and crisp.   *Makes 4 to 6 servings*

Hidden Valley® Cheese Fingers

2 small loaves (8 ounces each) French bread, cut in half
 lengthwise
1 package (8 ounces) cream cheese, softened
1 packet (1 ounce) HIDDEN VALLEY® The Original Ranch®
 Salad Dressing & Seasoning Mix
4 cups assorted toppings, such as chopped onions, bell
 peppers and shredded cheese

Slice bread crosswise into 1-inch fingers, leaving fingers attached to crust. Mix together cream cheese and salad dressing & seasoning mix. Spread on cut sides of bread. Sprinkle on desired toppings. Broil about 3 minutes or until brown and bubbly.   *Makes about 48 fingers*

Green Bean Casserole

Prep Time: 5 minutes   *Cook Time:* 30 minutes

1 envelope LIPTON® RECIPE SECRETS® Onion Mushroom
    Soup Mix
1 tablespoon all-purpose flour
1 cup milk
2 packages (10 ounces each) frozen cut green beans, thawed
1 cup shredded Cheddar cheese (about 4 ounces), divided
¼ cup plain dry bread crumbs

1. Preheat oven to 350°F. In 1½-quart casserole, combine soup mix, flour and milk; stir in green beans and ½ cup cheese.

2. Bake uncovered 25 minutes.

3. Sprinkle with bread crumbs and remaining ½ cup cheese. Bake an additional 5 minutes or until cheese is melted.

Makes 8 servings

Simple Savory Rice

Prep Time: 5 minutes   *Cook Time:* 25 minutes

2½ cups water
1 envelope LIPTON® RECIPE SECRETS® Soup Mix (any
    variety)
1 cup uncooked regular or converted rice

1. In 2-quart saucepan, bring water to a boil over high heat. Stir in soup mix and rice.

2. Reduce heat and simmer covered 20 minutes or until rice is tender.

Makes 3 servings

Vegetable Couscous

Prep Time: 5 minutes   *Cook Time:* 10 minutes

3 cups water
1 package KNORR® Recipe Classics™ Vegetable Soup,
    Dip and Recipe Mix
2 tablespoons BERTOLLI® Olive Oil or I CAN'T BELIEVE
    IT'S NOT BUTTER!® Spread
1 package (10 ounces) plain couscous (about 1½ cups)
¼ cup chopped fresh parsley (optional)
    Pine nuts, slivered almonds or raisins (optional)

• In 2-quart saucepan, bring water, recipe mix and olive oil to a boil, stirring frequently. Reduce heat; cover and simmer 2 minutes.

• Stir couscous into saucepan until evenly moistened. Remove from heat; cover and let stand 5 minutes.

• Fluff couscous with fork. Spoon into serving dish. Garnish, if desired, with chopped parsley and nuts or raisins.

Makes 5 cups couscous

Tip: Turn Vegetable Couscous into an easy one-dish meal. Just add 2 cups cut-up cooked chicken or turkey to the saucepan in step 1.

Creamed Spinach

Prep Time: 5 minutes   *Cook Time:* 10 minutes

2 cups milk
1 package KNORR® Recipe Classics™ Leek Soup, Dip and
    Recipe Mix
1 bag (16 ounces) frozen chopped spinach
⅛ teaspoon ground nutmeg

• In medium saucepan, combine milk and recipe mix. Bring to a boil over medium heat.

• Add spinach and nutmeg; stirring frequently. Bring to a boil over high heat. Reduce heat to low and simmer, stirring frequently, 5 minutes.

Makes 6 servings

Broccoli & Red Pepper Sauté

2 tablespoons olive or vegetable oil
4 cups small broccoli florets
1 large red bell pepper, cut into thin strips
1 medium onion, sliced
1 clove garlic, finely chopped
1 envelope LIPTON® RECIPE SECRETS® Golden Herb with
    Lemon Soup Mix*
1 cup water
¼ cup sliced almonds, toasted (optional)

**Also terrific with Lipton Recipe Secrets Savory Herb with Garlic
Soup Mix.*

In 12-inch skillet, heat oil over medium heat and cook broccoli,
red pepper, onion and garlic, stirring occasionally, 5 minutes or
until onion is tender. Add Golden Herb with Lemon Soup Mix
with water. Simmer covered 5 minutes or until broccoli is
tender. Sprinkle with almonds.   *Makes about 6 servings*

Garlic Fries

Prep Time: 5 minutes   *Cook Time:* 25 minutes

1 bag (32 ounces) frozen French fried potatoes
1 envelope LIPTON® RECIPE SECRETS® Savory Herb with
    Garlic Soup Mix*

*Also terrific with LIPTON® RECIPE SECRETS® Onion Soup Mix.

1. Preheat oven to 450°F. In large bowl, thoroughly toss frozen
French fried potatoes with soup mix; spread on jelly-roll pan.

2. Bake until golden and crisp, about 25 minutes, stirring once.
          Makes 4 servings

Scalloped Garlic Potatoes

3 medium all-purpose potatoes, peeled and thinly sliced
(about 1½ pounds)
1 envelope LIPTON® RECIPE SECRETS® Garlic Mushroom
Soup Mix*
1 cup (½ pint) whipping or heavy cream
½ cup water

*Also terrific with LIPTON® RECIPE SECRETS® Savory Herb with
Garlic Soup Mix.*

1. Preheat oven to 375°F. In lightly greased 2-quart shallow
baking dish, arrange potatoes. In medium bowl, blend
remaining ingredients; pour over potatoes.

2. Bake uncovered 45 minutes or until potatoes are tender.

Makes 4 servings

More Sweets, Please!

Frozen Black-Bottom-Peanut Butter Pie

Prep Time: 10 minutes plus freezing

37 RITZ® Crackers
6 tablespoons butter or margarine, melted
⅓ cup hot fudge dessert topping, heated slightly to soften
1 cup creamy peanut butter
1 cup cold milk
1 package (4-serving size) JELL-O® Vanilla *or* Chocolate Flavor Instant Pudding & Pie Filling
1 tub (8 ounces) COOL WHIP® Whipped Topping, thawed Chopped PLANTERS® Peanuts (optional)

CRUSH crackers in zipper-style plastic bag with rolling pin or in food processor. Mix cracker crumbs and butter. Press onto bottom and up side of 9-inch pie plate; chill. Carefully spread fudge topping over crust.

BEAT peanut butter and milk in large bowl with wire whisk until blended. Add pudding mix. Beat with wire whisk 2 minutes or until well blended. Stir in ½ tub whipped topping. Spoon into crust. Spread remaining whipped topping over top.

FREEZE 4 hours. Sprinkle with chopped PLANTERS® Peanuts. *Makes 8 servings*

Great Substitute: Try using chunky peanut butter instead of creamy for extra peanut flavor.

Easy Lemon Pudding Cookies

Prep Time: 10 minutes   *Bake Time:* 10 minutes

1 cup BISQUICK® Original Baking Mix
1 package (4-serving size) JELL-O® Lemon Flavor Instant
   Pudding & Pie Filling
½ teaspoon ground ginger (optional)
1 egg, lightly beaten
¼ cup vegetable oil
   Sugar
3 squares BAKER'S® Premium White Baking Chocolate,
   melted

HEAT oven to 350°F.

STIR baking mix, pudding mix and ginger in medium bowl. Mix
in egg and oil until well blended. (Mixture will be stiff.) With
hands, roll cookie dough into 1-inch diameter balls. Place balls
2 inches apart on lightly greased cookie sheets. Dip flat-bottom
glass into sugar. Press glass onto each dough ball and flatten
into ¼-inch-thick cookie.

BAKE 10 minutes or until edges are golden brown. Immediately
remove from cookie sheets. Cool on wire racks. Drizzle cookies
with melted white chocolate.   *Makes about 20 cookies*

How To Melt Chocolate: Microwave 3 squares BAKER'S®
Premium White Baking Chocolate in heavy zipper-style plastic
sandwich bag on HIGH 1 to 1½ minutes or until chocolate is
almost melted. Gently knead bag until chocolate is completely
melted. Fold down top of bag; snip tiny piece off 1 corner from
bottom. Holding top of bag tightly, drizzle chocolate through
opening across tops of cookies.

Jell-O® Yogurt Parfaits

Prep Time: 10 minutes plus refrigerating

2 cups boiling water, divided
1 package (4-serving size) JELL-O® Brand Gelatin, any red flavor
1 container (8 ounces) BREYERS® Vanilla Lowfat Yogurt, divided
1 cup cold water, divided
1 package (4-serving size) JELL-O® Brand Orange Flavor Gelatin

STIR 1 cup boiling water into red gelatin in medium bowl at least 2 minutes or until completely dissolved. Remove ½ cup gelatin to small bowl. Stir in ½ of the yogurt. Stir ½ cup cold water into other bowl. Refrigerate both bowls 15 to 20 minutes or until slightly thickened (consistency of unbeaten egg whites).

SPOON creamy red gelatin mixture evenly into 4 dessert glasses. Refrigerate 10 minutes or until thickened (spoon drawn through leaves a definite impression). Top each with clear red gelatin. Refrigerate until thickened.

MEANWHILE, repeat procedure with orange gelatin and remaining ingredients.

REFRIGERATE 3 hours or until firm.

GARNISH each serving with a dollop of thawed COOL WHIP® Whipped Topping. *Makes 4 servings*

Great Substitute: For a fun holiday treat, substitute Lime Flavor Gelatin for the Orange Flavor Gelatin.

Magic Cookie Bars

Prep Time: 10 minutes   *Bake Time:* 25 minutes

½ cup (1 stick) butter or margarine
1½ cups graham cracker crumbs
1 (14-ounce) can EAGLE® BRAND Sweetened Condensed
     Milk (NOT evaporated milk)
2 cups (12 ounces) semi-sweet chocolate chips
1⅓ cups flaked coconut
1 cup chopped nuts

1. Preheat oven to 350°F (325°F for glass dish). In 13×9-inch baking pan, melt butter in oven.

2. Sprinkle crumbs over butter; pour Eagle Brand evenly over crumbs. Layer evenly with remaining ingredients; press down firmly.

3. Bake 25 minutes or until lightly browned. Cool. Chill, if desired. Cut into bars. Store loosely covered at room temperature.   *Makes 2 to 3 dozen bars*

7-Layer Magic Cookie Bars: Substitute 1 cup (6 ounces) butterscotch-flavored chips* for 1 cup semi-sweet chocolate chips.

*Peanut butter-flavored chips or white chocolate chips can be substituted for butterscotch-flavored chips.

Magic Peanut Cookie Bars: Substitute 2 cups (about ¾ pound) chocolate-covered peanuts for semi-sweet chocolate chips and chopped nuts.

Magic Rainbow Cookie Bars: Substitute 2 cups plain candy-coated chocolate pieces for semi-sweet chocolate chips.

Top to bottom: Magic Cookie Bars,
Magic Rainbow Cookie Bars

Nutty Blueberry Muffins

1 package DUNCAN HINES® Bakery-Style Wild Maine
   Blueberry Muffin Mix
2 egg whites
½ cup water
⅓ cup chopped pecans

1. Preheat oven to 400°F. Grease 2½-inch muffin cups (or use paper liners).

Rinse blueberries from Mix with cold water and drain.

2. Pour muffin mix into large bowl. Break up any lumps. Add egg whites and water. Stir until moistened, about 50 strokes. Stir in pecans; gently fold in blueberries.

3. For large muffins, fill cups two-thirds full. Bake 17 to 22 minutes or until toothpick inserted in center comes out clean. (For medium muffins, fill cups half full. Bake 15 to 20 minutes.) Cool in pan 5 to 10 minutes. Loosen carefully before removing from pan.

Makes 8 large or 12 medium muffins

Tip: To reheat leftover muffins, wrap the muffins tightly in foil. Place them in a 400°F oven for 10 to 15 minutes.

Nutty Blueberry Muffins

Fudge Ribbon Cake

Prep Time: 20 minutes   *Bake Time:* 40 minutes

1 (18.25-ounce) package chocolate cake mix
1 (8-ounce) package cream cheese, softened
2 tablespoons butter or margarine, softened
1 tablespoon cornstarch
1 (14-ounce) can EAGLE® BRAND Sweetened Condensed
    Milk (NOT evaporated milk)
1 egg
1 teaspoon vanilla extract
    Chocolate Glaze (recipe follows)

1. Preheat oven to 350°F. Grease and flour 13×9-inch baking pan. Prepare cake mix as package directs. Pour batter into prepared pan.

2. In small mixing bowl, beat cream cheese, butter and cornstarch until fluffy. Gradually beat in Eagle Brand. Add egg and vanilla; beat until smooth. Spoon evenly over cake batter.

3. Bake 40 minutes or until wooden pick inserted near center comes out clean. Cool. Prepare Chocolate Glaze and drizzle over cake. Store covered in refrigerator.   *Makes 10 to 12 servings*

Chocolate Glaze: In small saucepan over low heat, melt 1 (1-ounce) square unsweetened or semi-sweet chocolate and 1 tablespoon butter or margarine with 2 tablespoons water. Remove from heat. Stir in ¾ cup powdered sugar and ½ teaspoon vanilla extract. Stir until smooth and well blended. Makes about ⅓ cup.

Fudge Ribbon Bundt Cake: Preheat oven to 350°F. Grease and flour 10-inch Bundt pan. Prepare cake mix as package directs. Pour batter into prepared pan. Prepare cream cheese layer as directed above; spoon evenly over batter. Bake 50 to 55 minutes or until wooden pick inserted near center comes out clean. Cool 10 minutes. Remove from pan. Cool. Prepare Chocolate Glaze and drizzle over cake. Store covered in refrigerator.

Top to bottom: Fudge Ribbon Cake,
Fudge Ribbon Bundt Cake

Cranberry Cobbler

2 (16-ounce) cans sliced peaches in light syrup, drained
1 (16-ounce) can whole berry cranberry sauce
1 package DUNCAN HINES® Cinnamon Swirl Muffin Mix
½ cup chopped pecans
⅓ cup butter or margarine, melted
   Whipped topping or ice cream

1. Preheat oven to 350°F.

2. Cut peach slices in half lengthwise. Combine peach slices and cranberry sauce in *ungreased* 9-inch square pan. Knead swirl packet from Mix for 10 seconds. Squeeze contents evenly over fruit.

3. Combine muffin mix, contents of topping packet from Mix and pecans in large bowl. Add melted butter. Stir until thoroughly blended (mixture will be crumbly). Sprinkle crumbs over fruit. Bake 40 to 45 minutes or until lightly browned and bubbly. Serve warm with whipped topping.   *Makes 9 servings*

Tip: Store leftovers in the refrigerator. Reheat in microwave oven to serve warm.

Philadelphia® Cheesecake Brownies

Prep time: 20 minutes   *Bake time:* 40 minutes

1 package (19.8 ounces) brownie mix (do not use mix that
   includes syrup pouch)
1 package (8 ounces) PHILADELPHIA® Cream Cheese,
   softened
⅓ cup sugar
1 egg
½ teaspoon vanilla

PREPARE brownie mix as directed on package. Pour into greased 13×9-inch baking pan.

BEAT cream cheese with electric mixer on medium speed until smooth. Mix in sugar until blended. Add egg and vanilla; mix just until blended. Pour cream cheese mixture over brownie batter; cut through batter with knife several times for marble effect.

BAKE at 350°F for 35 to 40 minutes or until cream cheese mixture is lightly browned. Cool. Cut into squares.

Makes 2 dozen brownies

Special Extras: For extra chocolate flavor, sprinkle 1 cup BAKER'S® Semi-Sweet Real Chocolate Chunks over top of brownies before baking.

Sparkling Fruit Tart

Prep Time: 15 minutes plus refrigerating

1 cup boiling water
1 package (4-serving size) JELL-O® Brand Strawberry Flavor
  Gelatin
1 package (10 ounces) frozen strawberries in syrup
1 can (11 ounces) mandarin orange segments, drained
1 small banana, sliced
1 HONEY MAID® Honey Graham Pie Crust (9 inch)

STIR boiling water into gelatin in large bowl at least 2 minutes until completely dissolved. Add frozen strawberries. Stir until strawberries thaw and gelatin becomes slightly thickened (consistency of unbeaten egg whites).

ARRANGE orange and banana slices on bottom crust. Carefully spoon gelatin mixture over fruit.

REFRIGERATE 4 hours or until firm. Garnish with thawed COOL WHIP® Whipped Topping and fresh strawberry fans, if desired.   *Makes 8 to 10 servings*

Chewy Fruit & Nut Bars

Prep Time: 15 minutes plus refrigerating

2 cups LORNA DOONE® Shortbread crumbs
5 tablespoons butter or margarine, melted
1 cup boiling water
2 packages (4-serving size each) JELL-O® Brand Apricot
    or Peach Flavor Gelatin
½ cup light corn syrup
1 cup chopped toasted PLANTERS® Slivered Almonds

STIR crumbs and butter in 9-inch square baking pan until crumbs are well moistened, reserving ½ cup crumb mixture. Firmly press remaining crumbs onto bottom of pan. Refrigerate until ready to fill.

STIR boiling water into gelatin in large bowl at least 2 minutes until completely dissolved. Stir in corn syrup. Refrigerate 15 minutes or until slightly thickened (consistency of unbeaten egg whites). Stir in almonds. Pour into pan over crust. Sprinkle with remaining crumbs.

REFRIGERATE 3 hours or until firm. Cut into bars.

Makes 20 bars

Great Substitute: Use JELL-O® Brand Orange Flavor Gelatin instead of Apricot Flavor. Reduce almonds to ½ cup and add ½ cup chopped dried apricots.

Acknowledgments

The publisher would like to thank the companies and organizations listed below for the use of their recipes and photographs in this publication.

Birds Eye®

ConAgra Foods®

Duncan Hines® and Moist Deluxe® are registered

trademarks of Aurora Foods Inc.

Eagle® Brand

The Golden Grain Company®

The Hidden Valley® Food Products Company

Kraft Foods Holdings

Lawry's® Foods, Inc.

Norseland, Inc. / Lucini Italia Co.

Uncle Ben's Inc.

Unilever Bestfoods North America

METRIC CONVERSION CHART

VOLUME MEASUREMENTS (dry)

$\frac{1}{8}$ teaspoon = 0.5 mL
$\frac{1}{4}$ teaspoon = 1 mL
$\frac{1}{2}$ teaspoon = 2 mL
$\frac{3}{4}$ teaspoon = 4 mL
1 teaspoon = 5 mL
1 tablespoon = 15 mL
2 tablespoons = 30 mL
$\frac{1}{4}$ cup = 60 mL
$\frac{1}{3}$ cup = 75 mL
$\frac{1}{2}$ cup = 125 mL
$\frac{2}{3}$ cup = 150 mL
$\frac{3}{4}$ cup = 175 mL
1 cup = 250 mL
2 cups = 1 pint = 500 mL
3 cups = 750 mL
4 cups = 1 quart = 1 L

VOLUME MEASUREMENTS (fluid)

1 fluid ounce (2 tablespoons) = 30 mL
4 fluid ounces ($\frac{1}{2}$ cup) = 125 mL
8 fluid ounces (1 cup) = 250 mL
12 fluid ounces (1$\frac{1}{2}$ cups) = 375 mL
16 fluid ounces (2 cups) = 500 mL

WEIGHTS (mass)

$\frac{1}{2}$ ounce = 15 g
1 ounce = 30 g
3 ounces = 90 g
4 ounces = 120 g
8 ounces = 225 g
10 ounces = 285 g
12 ounces = 360 g
16 ounces = 1 pound = 450 g

DIMENSIONS

$\frac{1}{16}$ inch = 2 mm
$\frac{1}{8}$ inch = 3 mm
$\frac{1}{4}$ inch = 6 mm
$\frac{1}{2}$ inch = 1.5 cm
$\frac{3}{4}$ inch = 2 cm
1 inch = 2.5 cm

OVEN TEMPERATURES

250°F = 120°C
275°F = 140°C
300°F = 150°C
325°F = 160°C
350°F = 180°C
375°F = 190°C
400°F = 200°C
425°F = 220°C
450°F = 230°C

BAKING PAN SIZES

Utensil	Size in Inches/Quarts	Metric Volume	Size in Centimeters
Baking or Cake Pan (square or rectangular)	8×8×2	2 L	20×20×5
	9×9×2	2.5 L	23×23×5
	12×8×2	3 L	30×20×5
	13×9×2	3.5 L	33×23×5
Loaf Pan	8×4×3	1.5 L	20×10×7
	9×5×3	2 L	23×13×7
Round Layer Cake Pan	8×1½	1.2 L	20×4
	9×1½	1.5 L	23×4
Pie Plate	8×1¼	750 mL	20×3
	9×1¼	1 L	23×3
Baking Dish or Casserole	1 quart	1 L	—
	1½ quart	1.5 L	—
	2 quart	2 L	—